DAWN DANCING

A Collection of Poetry

By
Elaine Webster

Published by: the Institute for Economic Democracy Press
2010
Sun City, Arizona, USA
888.533.1020 / www.ied.info / ied@ied.info

In Cooperation with the Institute on World Problems
www.worldproblems.net

Dawn Dancing – Version 1.0

Library of Congress Cataloging-in-Publication Data

Webster, Elaine, 1942-
Dawn Dancing : a collection of poetry / by Elaine Webster.
p. cm.
Published in cooperation with the Institute on World Problems.
ISBN 978-1-933567-28-0 (alk. paper)
I. Title.
PS3623.E3964D39 2009
811'.6--dc22

2009047559

Book cover designed by Michelle Macirella.

This book is printed on acid free paper.

OTHER BOOKS BY ELAINE WEBSTER

Seeking Balance
Grandma's In The Basement

DEDICATION

To, Barb, dear friend, colleague and mentor.
When we said our good-byes, after a walk by the lake,
I did not know it would be our last meeting.
Cancer can be such an insidious enemy.

I thank you for all you taught me and am
sending my appreciation to you through this book.

BARB

I remember our first meeting
sharing poems
sunlight beaming
on surrounding plants
encircling us with caring.

Hours spent re-writing, cut and paste
always patient
guiding smile
creating my wings
birthing a new author of poesy.

Walks along the lake sparkling
gentle ripples
eroded shoreline
sharing ideas
overhead gulls calling.

Memories linger of our last lunch
picture taking
continued support
with latest writing
warm smiles over ice cream.

Warm sunlight shelters us
during fond good-byes
until we meet again.

ACKNOWLEDGMENTS

I would like to thank my good friend, Glen Martin, my son-in-law, Scott Broberg and my daughter, Michelle Macirella. They continue to give me a great deal of support and technical guidance. In Michelle's case, credit goes to her for this wonderful book cover. The photo is from her collection and can be seen on her website, along with other sample photos listed in her galleries, at www.luminariaphotography.com.

PREFACE

The following three poems were written by Dr. Glen T. Martin. He is a life-long friend and amazing humanitarian. It is imperative for me to include his poems and lead the reader to his website. (www.radford.edu/gmartin) His dedication and tireless work in helping to promote a World Wide Government Organization, at this time, speaks volumes. It is a testament of his character and to this planet's need for unity.

This Grey Dawn

Glen T. Martin

25 July 2003

The fire in my bones receding now,
        as I approach the rainy arc,
                and slowly drift toward the last good night;

As I turn my face to unknown years,
        of hope and struggle,
                that animate my past and present;

And experience each day fading into night,
        And night to another day,
                this grey dawn awakens a solitary reflection -

How shall I use this new day,
        this moment that drifts,
                into the diurnal round,

Like a dream,
        like the flight of a nightingale,
                into the darkening woods of evening;

What do I know?
        How must I act?
                What may I hope?

These eternal inquiries,
        of the philosophic quest,
                emerge in deep disquiet;

As the fire from within no longer burns,
        out of control, an irresistible internal combustion,
                        its own reason for being.

The fire flickers now,
fades unexpectedly,
grows bright again, then dim,

Reducing day by day the hope and struggle,
to dying embers, flickering coals,
ashes fading to the dark of night;

Today's new dawn,
with this dark forest beside my cabin,
and this shining lake before me like a jewel,

Will not rise again,
with assurance and bravado,
as when the fire in my bones was all;

The morning grows to daylight,
brief hours of work and effort, energy
and accomplishment, less each day

This fire in my bones receding now,
in years that bring the philosophic mind,
does not inspire an ode on immortality;

My heart is moved this grey morning,
as I approach the rainy arc,
by turns to weariness and hope,

A poet from my youth,
speaks to me again in a different voice,
here upon this distant shore -

"How shall I use these dangling hands,
these feet of mine that draw me on like dreams?"

FREEDOM

16 August 2004

What is this freedom that beckons at the door,
And opens to the heart in moments rare?
What is this song, that comes from bards of yore,
Teaching the fragrance of a purer air,
Than daily care, and fret, and thoughts so poor?

I know there is another bliss,
Beyond the beauty of a woman's kiss,
A bliss that intimates our future state,
Of peace beyond recalling, ne'er too late
To vibrate in the god, an affirmation of our fate.

I watch the stars at night, the inky black,
Bespeckled by a million points of light,
And know the destiny of humankind,
As truth and freedom from the daily grind,
A wafting in this wind of bliss and might.

This awareness of the sparkling world,
Reflected in the limpid mind,
Responding deeply to its kind,
In bird and tree and sky and sea –
This freedom-world was made for me.

The Alchemist's Song
Glen T. Martin
1990

"Der Goldmacher is der einzige wahre Wohlthater der Menscheit."
- Nietzsche

The simple shining of the world's presence leaps forth in the alchemic Now of hope:
transfiguring immediacy into fire,
changing darkness into light.

We have seen –
that knowledge cannot save, and founders in the despair of crumbling centuries:
discarded beliefs, lost paradigms flowing forever pastward,
towards oblivion, into dark.

We have seen –
values, and the terrified face, struggle for the future listless against a backdrop
of realities no longer believed, no longer loved –
disintegrating toward the twilight of unreality and myth.

And the centuries pound forward, adamant,
pressing us dark against the unknown face,
relentless – knowledge cannot save,
merciless – values do not sustain;

And we have seen ourselves –
belonging wholly nowhere,
in the dark of the unknown face – alone.

Yet the simple shining of the world's presence leaps forth in the alchemic Now of hope!
and a fire scintillates even in this stillness!

It bursts forth shimmering, a silent spectrum of unknown sparks –
Despair dissolved in the great world work, even now.

And we see –
emptiness shine forth its inner light,
beyond knowing, the golden glow breaking fast,
brilliant between concepts –
in radiance the silent paradigms surpassed.

And we see –
the simple shining of the world-presence,
embrace our being-in-the-world,
and lift us gently toward the sacred ceremony of hope,

The Eschaton breaks forth, redeeming value in the unknown light
of the alchemic face, radiant in mystery,
gathering again the world,
and promising transfiguration –
Our Transformation – in the simple shining of the holy fire.

The world to be, beyond the nothingness of knowledge and utility,
leaps forth that radiant face,
in the alchemic light beyond being,
that purifying pyre –

That world leaps forth, beyond the dingy paths of everyday,
out of the sacred silence of our being,
and toward the alchemic mystery of the living moment,
a fire in our Now, until that Now is all.

TABLE OF CONTENTS

Just For Fun

Ruminations

Raquette Lake, NY – Adirondacks

Italy – Greece

Florida

Political Questions

Epilogue

JUST FOR FUN

...cats behind screen
in pounce position
all enjoying summer day

SWEAT

Skinny running man
skin flapping
rear bouncing
feet pounding
down the street

WANT COMPANY?

Hey handsome guy
stopped at light
moon roof open
head tilted back
wide orgasmic smile
greeting the sunshine

PRECARIOUS BALANCE

Robust blind lady
juggles cane
soda can
in one hand
other hand gropes
for crossing button
on light pole
at street corner

SUMMER YEARNING

Jiggling boob girl
still beaded wet
from her swim
feet on sand
move towards
her man
he straddles rock
thrust straight up
from lake's edge
their arms entwine
wet skin
warm sun
my skin prickles
with a similar memory
tears gather on cheeks

PITTSFORD VILLAGE

Bald angry man
screaming at tree
banging his head
against rough bark
outside pizza parlor

FRIEND SCOTT

Cute daughter's beau
quick steps
on treadmill
reading book
on phone
big smile
listening to my poems

PATIO TV

Chipper chipmunk perched
on rock ledge
tail in motion
side to side
mouth packed full
cats behind screen
in pounce position
all enjoying summer day

LAZY SUMMER DAY

Chubby bottom woodchuck
half hidden
in grass
at roadside
nibbling leaf
larger than his head

RUMINATIONS

Sunlight becomes a beacon
dancing its way
to my feet
it numbs the mind with beauty

DAWN DANCING

Who is the "I" that watches the mind
rise and set each day? A constant
dialog ensues in each
waking moment.

A question I ponder
as the pink glow
of dawn makes its journey
over the mountain tops.

Crystallized mist slithers
slowly up from
the mirrored lake
steam rising.

Sunlight becomes a beacon
dancing its way
to my feet
it numbs the mind with beauty.

KISSES TO THE WIND

I know it sounds naive my friend told the group
but all you really need is love. His love for wife
and daughters lit up the room.
He loved the land believed
in community. We shared a vision.

Sanctuary for mind body spirit
roaming freely with the buffies.
A name fondly given to the majestic
creatures on his farm. Yesterday
we shared our dreams with passion.

His hopes for the future energized all
he met and encouraged awareness
of inner peace. We wept together,
laughed and planned a future.
He was my adopted brother.

Now signals comfort me, a red cardinal peers
into my window. A hawk signals me in flight.
Feathers fall in my path. His smile enters my
meditation. Earth resonates with my tears as I mourn
his passing while feeling his presence

blow gentle kisses to the wind.

WALKING DOGS

Six deer stand
in tribute to fear.
White tails signal
my arrival.

Necks stretch
with cautious gaze,
watching from
behind the trees.

THE TRICKSTER

His posture   howling greeting
soft velvet ears at high alert.
Hiding behind nearest obstacle
we wait each other out.

Playing in the language   of canine.
Memories of your brother Ruble   ambush
locked front paws and human hands in combat.
We rolled to the ground.

A mix of laughter and growls   settled
on forest's soft flooring. Peering eyes
watch from distance. Fox   deer
connect with our moment.

What joy you brought to my heart,
sweet Alex. Your tricks surprised
my visits. Now you join Ruble
in another realm   smelling

each other in affectionate nuzzling
sparks a reunion. I carry you both
in my heart dear pups.   Antics
of my dear friend.

LITTLE DOG

from Virginia.....Pierre
in his name. Ancient
and wobbly, my shadow
he became.

My companion in the mountains
whimpering his commands -
need to pee, feed me now,
turn the night light on now, Ma'am.

We hiked the trails....me picking
him up when changing the lead.
Setting his short and chubby body
down again, he would pick up speed.

We ate meals together, watched
storms roll in and shivered in the
cold night air. That was my time spent
with little dog named Pierre.

SELLING TREES

I sit among the Scotch Pine
        and Douglas Fir while they
wait for a new home. Tis the season

to be jolly. Stoically, they stand
        branches wide and tall.
Can't resist hugging them.

Pine scent fills my nostrils
        resin sticks to my hands.
Smiling customers add energy

to this ritualistic gathering.
        I pee in a paint bucket
behind a tree while watching

the sun part the clouds above.
        There is magic in the air,
the trees and I can feel it. Night

joins me in dance when
        the generator lights up the sky.
The stream sounds louder at

night fall. The trees seem bigger. Bitter
        cold seeps into my limbs. Silence swallows
our pleasure. Tis the season to be jolly.

SUNFLOWERS

Sunflowers bend in sorrow
where once
they stood
tall

Blinding yellow smiles
reflected Joy
while reaching
upward

A seedling discovers
warm sunshine
and rain
drops

Change of season
returns all
to mother
earth

Change of time
catches up
with nature's
child

Sing joyous praise
and join
hands with
creation

THE PURPOSE

of a flower evokes
heady sense of euphoria
for me.

It is a fairy beckoning me
to skip through fields of blooming
colors and exotic smells.

Feet never touch the ground
as stems and velvet petals slip
through my toes.

Endless hue and aroma
easily sooth sadness
tripping my steps.

I make a chain of posies
that entangle my long blond hair
while dancing in the wind.

HIS TRUTH

I have this beautiful little boy
he said, while hands
lovingly caressed
empty air.

A smiling boy appeared in my
mind's eye, looking up
adoringly towards
his father.

A man swimming in pain
with courage, standing before
his friends
in Truth.

His truth, naked for all to see
a man
stood free
giving love.

Facing overwhelming fears
this man, was radiating
trust, beauty
Unconditional Love.

MISSING YOU

Sometimes, it is as if
you are right here
I can curl up
in your arms
to feel your heart
beat

But, it is my own heart
beating
in the missing…

TO DON AND HIS BRIDE

Faded snapshot with wrinkled edges.
Cousin Don smiling while holding me
in his arms. I, wearing the Shirley Temple
look, am enamored. Memories linger

of Don's ability to convince me
coins can disappear before my trusting eyes.
Laughter echoes from relentless teasing.

Fondness cements years of separate ways.
His smile is my aunt's smile I long to see again.
"I have met a wonderful woman," Don told me.
Enter stage left, the beautiful, Diana.

Her spirit and charm a mirror image of Don.
Dinner at Sardi's proved magical with Don, Diana
and daughter, Michelle. Three hours sizzled an

amazing connection. Warm hugs good-bye signaled
time to move on. Diana looked into Don's eyes
with a school girl adoration. Heading down Broadway
arm-in-arm, their notes of laughter joined

the evening's melodies. A new favorite photo
fresh in my mind. Two artists of life creating a
masterpiece. My cousin Don and his love, Diana,

weave a new pattern into the magnificent Journey
they are about to share. Just as the tenderness of a dove's
snowy wing soothes one's spirit, so their love will soar.
Much love and Congratulations!

AUNT MADELINE

At my father's funeral,
You hugged me and said,
"You need to cry, honey"
"You'll feel better."

When I was little,
I hugged my doll
Playing happily in
your back yard.

While growing up
we laughed together
Until the tears rolled
down our cheeks.

Joined in song with my mom
your melodies drifted heavenward
I sang Shirley Temple style
Love joined the rhythm.

Bowling, playing games
painting beautiful pictures
Fond memories dance joyously
through years flying by.

"We had a good life," you said
nearing the end
as we looked at photos
from the past.

As you grew older
solitude became
the chosen path
Your good nature remained a friend.

Near life's end, you lived in
a separate world
Seeing things that were not there
hearing voices where none were spoken.

Reaching out to say good-bye
I feel your hug
A gentle kiss, and a whispered
"I love you, honey."

"You were always such
a good girl."
"You're so beautiful."
"No boyfriend yet?"

I can feel your frail hands
on my face
Hear your tired mind
Trying to remember.

Peace came quietly
into your room
Your words caress my sadness
"You need to cry, honey."
"You'll feel better."

EVER REMINDED

What lurks behind this garb
of flesh
A battleground for thought
and silence

The mask of illusions
creates the need
Spirit gently cradles
the wounded

I sit at the edge
emerged in life
Surrounded by silent tombs
ever reminded

Closely linked to God's love
and patience
While struggling to quiet
the fires that rage.

HOLY MESSENGER

Beautiful wind.
        Holy Messenger
of change.

Howling continues
        through endless night
into the morn. I wake
to leafy colors bent
in submission
        from your strength.

This same strength
        carries me towards
the sky's playground
as I guide my plane
into a hungry thermal
        and spiral upward.

Circling in ascending motion
        your sound becomes
my compass for speed.
It is my direction and friend.
A mighty power
        directing my course.

Your message
        heralds the passing
of gentle breezes
calming the storm.
Descending into solitude,
        I am grounded.

Beautiful wind.
        Holy Messenger
of change.

STEPPING THROUGH

bedroom door opens memories
hidden away
I can't find the manual
entitled
“Growing Old Gracefully.”

Pictures positioned on bureau
walls
smile back at me
each one in freeze frame
recording history.

Somewhere along the way
I became invisible.

GRIPPED

in the jaws of my
unknown captor.
Muscles remain tense
as if with rigor mortis.

I drag this carcass
through time
wearing a carefree posture
a smile pasted onto my face.

A young girl, naive
as a new puppy
trusting the warmth
of each moment.

Sighs of exhaustion
billow skyward
knocking all down
in its path.

Breath is the answer
unlocking these binding chains.
It calms the raging shackles
allowing each moment to arrive.

REBIRTH

It is five a.m.
        pain is overwhelming
                shoulder and head throb
with dizzying lengths of despair, tears flow
                while sitting with my aloneness

A look at truth
        bargaining with the unknowable
                teaches lessons
Progress continues on my enlightened path
                or possible illusion

Forgiving, choices, accepting place
        in an unknown universe
                brings pangs of consciousness
Old friends and habits slip away
                I have shed the skin of another rebirth

WHILE WALKING

a young woman appeared
on my path one day.
She asked me about wisdom.
I offered her the word “choice”.
It will govern your life
bringing great sorrow
sandwiched with untold Joy.

TODAY I SAY GOOD-BYE

my dear furry friends
two dogs holding me enamored
with their antics
                    and love.

Chase circles the table
when I arrive, then backs
his rear into my leg
                    for butt scratches.

His Husky white fur is
thick and huggable, topped
with plush velvet ears – a stoic
                    with a hint of clown.

Carly is the energizing pup overflowing
with sweetness and mischief
her black lab intelligence
                    scans the room for chew toys.

A table, a chair or the wall
she is fine with gnawing on whatever is nearby
digging two foot holes or licking windowed doors.
                    Creative play with her unsuspecting brother
provides entertainment for me and invokes laughter.

Soon they travel west with family, adventure bound.
Their energy settles in around me while
fetching memories remain endless
                    soothing the loss.

toward our cabin in the woods.
My feline companion, Cinnamon
        and I, are eager
for our next adventure.

Fifteen years we have traveled
together. A year in Florida
        a small house in the country -
different locations brought delightful surprises.

We tried catching a mouse at 4 am.
She learned to climb a ladder to our sleeping loft.
        Hours spent with her
and favorite toy mouse, curled up in my lap,

while I typed or ate a meal.
The warm soft bundle
        purring her content.
Kidney failure ended her life – I mourn her loss.

The continual cycle of Loss and Joy is a double edged sword
bathed in honey. How sweet the tears
        that bring me closure
gently moving me forward.

RAQUETTE LAKE, NY ~ ADIRONDACKS

...surrounding me with peace
unimagined. My wish,
for this same gift, to blanket the world.

6:20 a.m.

heaven came calling
my way today
as dawn rose
over the lake.

Loons whaling lulled
me to sleep
while the forest
cradled my heart.

Subtle chirping mingled
with musical warbling,
rustling through the trees.
A milky mist

kisses the face of blue
over my head.
Dizzy with aroma of pine
stillness hangs loudly,

surrounding me with peace
unimagined. My wish,
for this same gift, to
blanket the world.

MEMORIES OF

open camp

Adirondack style

perched

on the hillside

overlooking

our lake

Years have accumulated
through layers
of summers
spent by its campfire

Lovers

once breathing
familiar wood smoke
permeating worn sleeping bags
this aroma drifts

unnoticed

As do the misquotes
buzzing by for dinner

near

flickering light
raccoons nimbly follow

trail

past couple entwined

in the moment

HAIKU MOMENT

The morning chatter
increases with rising sun
my Joy escalates

winged creatures in flight
join the frogs croaking loudly
sounds echo off pond

into open heart
wide with the wonder of Now
in tune with earth's song

THE SPRING

Raptured melodies bubble
to the surface
of the spring.

Hidden among upturned roots
mighty pines downed
in stormy battle.

Cool water soothes my throat
lily pads nearby in full bloom
calm my vision.

Tail thunderously slapping
echoes throughout
my secret cove.

Great dams border stream entrance
quick splash details
where beavers are swimming.

Haunting cry from hawk
swooping over my sanctuary
overshadow the mysterious loon.

Nearby, deer ankle deep at water's edge
share my wonder
by the spring.

PIPE CEREMONY

We gently glide our vessel
through the water lilies
A duck follows
        back to camp while
feeding a lone fish   crumbs
        floating downward

Reverently we glide our feet
over fallen trees   colored leaves
which cover our path
        collecting white birch
Admiring golden clusters of fungi
        sprouting upward

Chosen spot on rock cliff
leads us to mossy edge
Looking over lake's view
        and down   into rays
of sunshine from summer's
        last visit

He prepared pipe ceremony
sweet sage cleansed our hearts
feathering my spirit to fly
        while grandfathers   smile down
Sending messengers
        with their blessings

One immense golden butterfly appeared
over the rim of our perch
It brought us answer
        of Joy   Transformation   then danced
into our opening hearts   bringing peace
        with awareness

Two friends sharing this moment
grateful for insight sent
Warm breeze assures
          guides   are present
Ancient truths emerge from sacred
          pipe ceremony

BEAVER BROOK

Three travelers set out for adventure.
It was evening   the moon was full.
Our small craft quietly maneuvered
around   and through   the brook's
long inviting artery.

Making a pact   we agreed neither
to use a flashlight   or engage in conversation.
Evening's bright light guided us.
Anticipation   and mystery   became fuel
for our thoughts.

Dead tree stumps loomed as monsters.
Sudden wings flapping   followed by
long neck creatures circling in the air.
Glowing   eyes appeared   at each bend
watching passing visitors.

First beaver dam ahead.
Water rushes   over huge
wooden structure ahead.
Silently   we slid   canoe over
continuing on into the unknown ahead.

WE CIRCLED

by the campfire
  for a pipe ceremony.
Distant owl signals
  unseen sage.

Ancient Grandfathers nod approval
  amongst the forest.
Loon cries startle the night
  awakening my inner heart.

Friendship causes
  this gathering.
Prayers ask to be heard
  under evenings splendor.

Sounds from distant jazz trumpet dance
  across the lake, entering
this reverent moment.
  Smiles skip around the circle..

Bass-throated bull frogs
  add to the chorus.
Joining hands in praise,
  we give thanks to creation.

THE CRAGS

have become a looming legend.
Footsteps along the wooded
trail pass succulent mushrooms growing
on logs plush with green furry moss.

White birch line the way towards base
of grandfather boulders reaching
massively tall. A narrow ledge allows
our passage upward.

It leads us ever higher
through crack found near knurled
tree roots along the ledge. Our entrance
to the top emerges.

Arriving upon the velvet covered
stone shelf, the lake below signals
this new world.   Signs
of other creatures are evident

with each step taken   through
high grass and under fallen
pine trunks. Morning dew hangs as if a
diamond necklace on spun webs.

To view the world from this height takes
breath away   exhaling
with wonder.   Peace becomes the cloak
worn on descent.

PARALLEL FLOWERING

Pen in hand I begin to see, through this form of vision
  A parallel history flowering as I age wisely
One can only hope it is with grace
Dignity, fills my heart
Guiding me into the mystery whether I should ask for it
  or wish it to dissipate
I am amongst the vapors of time
  that bring me home
          to my blossoming

II

Why does this parallel history bring sadness to my heart?
  I see the ghosts of yesterday holding hands with my present
They are dancing arm and arm into my future
Gasping for breath - yet, dizzy with Joy
Smells of balsam, campfire smoke, clear mountain lake lulls me
  Into receptive prayer of thanksgiving, gratitude and wonderment
Truth caresses my being
  as the wind gently massages
          my soul in transition

WIND WHISTLES

Dusk falls on spider's web
  bringing silence
    to our campfire
crackling a warm welcome
    into the night.

The web hangs loosely
  between logs of open camp
    its design so intense,
as if made
    by master weavers.

Wind whistles through
  the pines, reminiscent of a car
    racing past our view.
The forest becomes alive
    with strengthening storm.

Flying shadows dart among the trees.
  Sonar driven bats
    race along the water's edge.
The spider remains
    engrossed in its task.

Pine branches bend
  with the rushing wind.
    Our quiet evening
erupts into the starry brilliance above
    warnings of the advancing rain.

EYES OF VISION

It is another damp and drizzling morning
in the mountains
The air hangs moist
the bugs are having a field day
with my blood

The words choice and responsibility
hover over the horizon
Making bitterness and blaming
sink into the shimmering light
reaching across the lake

If one is truly present, we see
with eyes of vision
Awareness we may not want to face
while learning to love
and accept ourselves

I AM SITTING

in my cabin perched a few feet from the ledge overlooking the lake.
The large screened front wall window is framed by evergreens cleverly attached
to the earth outside. My view is the mountains sloping towards each other, yet,
running in different directions. They form a range of green-leaf beauty.
It rained during the early dawn and now mist is rolling off the lake and drifting
across my vision.

The full moon hung huge in the clouds last night. Its reflection skipped over to my
door step. The beckoning loon calls echoed throughout the night. This has been
a delightful weekend filled with political discussions, boat rides, campfire, hikes,
swimming, walk to the spring – all shared with friends and family.

Just returned from the outhouse on the hill. Carefully stepping over huge mounds
of deer remains, I made my way through collected leaves and twigs. They lay
in a weaved pattern made over many years. Rain drops gently caress my hair
on my journey. Pink Floyd runs through my mind, playing from my MP3
clipped to my shirt.

Sitting on the sacred throne with the door opened to my wooded court, I am reminded
how powerful NOW really is and give in to the Joy.

ITALY ~ GREECE

...my mind drifts to the splendor
that was Rome and seek refuge
in the garden.

MY SIESTA

lingers long
while wine plays
with my mind.

Outside the villa
humming from water pump
brings vision

of daughter's first splash
in bathroom tub.
Sunlight spills onto tiled floor.

Yellow lemons and
sumptuous figs hang from their branches.
Tomatoes and fresh pasta lay drying.

WHAT BEAUTY

Che Bella   Che Bella
"What beauty"   resounded
through the tunnel where trains
arrive and depart. Outstretched arms
passed my baby wrapped in pink

over their heads for an eager glimpse
of the new born. Brakes screeching
smoke funneling upwards. Travelers
scurrying in this foreign land.
Watching my child's journey and

cry of bewilderment produced tears.
We had just traveled from Switzerland
to Bari on an overnight. Sharing
an upper berth with infant tucked securely
near my heart. Voices in unison

out of sync   each shouting their own
greeting. Welcome to Italy and all its charm.
Relatives anxious to share their homes
their culture dating back to BC   laced
in pain and royal splendor.

SCENTED CLOUD

Shrill sounds of the cock's crow
  jolted me into a waking state.
Laying in a strange bed with warm
  starched sheets still wrinkled

in a ball by my feet.
Roosters have no mercy.

A scented cloud of Jasmine
  floats through my window.
It soothes my waking mind
  reminding me of yesterday's

lunch in the garden while
Mt. Etna spouted red lava on horizon.

SHOPPING WITH THE GODFATHER

We scurried to keep up
daughter and I   a few paces
behind the Godfather   our uncle,
shopping was the purpose.

Soldiers behind their sergeant,
obeying each command.   Uncle gave
out the orders   shop here   buy this
we then marched on to yet,

another store. His heart full
of kindness   no time to dawdle
no questions answered. Choice of stores provided
meant, pick a gift graciously.   Grazie, Zio.

Always time for a quick cappuccino and biscuit
at nearby seaside restaurant. Godfather spoke
of the glorious day with hands gesturing
his every word as if conducting an orchestra.

We then sped through the narrow streets
in his shiny sports car. Mission accomplished
as we raced home to the villa   a fortress
of strength and love waited our return.

GATED VILLA

Pacing perimeter of gated villa
guard dogs bare their teeth.
Warning, stay away from master's

domain. Skin tightly drawn over
their rib cage. Hungry for scraps given at
noon meal, barking continues

throughout the night. Broken bottles and
barbed wire lay on top of cement walls
surrounding each home.

Owners sumptuously eat figs while
basking in morning's sunshine by the sea.

REFUGE IN THE GARDEN

Before entering the villa, I must give my name.
Once inside the gate, follow path through the garden
passing a pond full of ornamental Chinese gold fish.
Droplets spray down from golden fountain
onto orange and red colored fins rippling
reminiscent of oriental fans in slow motion.

Standing in the foyer built for a giant,
marble gleams from beneath my feet.
Staircase reaches up endlessly towards cathedral dome.
Gold bathroom fixtures beam light through doorway.
An Italian feast with relatives awaits.
The guests treated like royal crown jewels.

Dinner on the patio continues into the night as does the heated conversation.
Father against son in political battle square off
while we eat at ten foot long tiled table.
Father's beliefs argue son's communist thinking, enraged he
starts beating son with his shoe. My mind drifts
to the splendor that was Rome and seek refuge in the garden.

SILENT POWER

The enormity of his body
was beyond my
comprehension.
He lay in a prone position,
resting.

Hair flowed gracefully
from his entire structure.
Hands were
large enough to sit in.
Curious eyes gazed into mine.

Thirty minutes in total
astonishment, needed
to walk around
this amazing primate
named King Kong.

He ruled the screen
traversing buildings in
large cities.
Now he rules the museum
with silent power.

Nestled in the foothills
by the coastal town
of Riminee.
Italy hosts a treasure gently speaking
to those who will listen.

MY HEART SOARED WITH GRATITUDE

Steady drips repeatedly rolled off the boat's oars
  sending drops into the briny sea,
interrupting the silence.

We bent heads in prayer position
  and rowed into the cave.
An iridescent deep blue glow surrounded our vessel.

These same beaded drips echoed
  our arrival into the Blue Grotto.
Awe replaced unspoken words of wonder.

How often have I sat by the raging sea
  dreaming of peace? Dreaming of silence?
Today it opened its arms and swallowed me.

Floating through an inner passage
  of reflected blue walls,
I overflow with gratitude.

BIRDS SINGING MELODIES

A tree branch on nearby hill stretches out
towards the ground's   aging cavernous opening.
Birds sing melodies where   lions roared
over cries of Christians slain   for sport.

Eroding granite seats all in a row
form an oval around   gaping hole.
Missing floor   once covered small rooms
where victims and warriors waited for battle.

Traffic flows freely around this structure   passing
arch leading to the Forum. Here, ancient
Government decreed laws of the day.   Nearby,
chariot races   added to the ancient cries

of fear and death. Birds sing melodies.
Glorious flowers bloom. Another splendor
that was Rome   looms tall
slowly fading with time.   Yet,

standing near the wall's edge   viewing
this massive structure,   time meets time
in questioning wonder.   Silence   allows vision
of destruction to appear.

HAUNTING MELODY

Erect remains of Acropolis
  loom high amongst fallen stone.
Whispering sounds of ancient legislature
  delivering their laws

still lingers in the haze.
Echoing through remaining pillars
  and over boulder once holding St. Paul's feet
    as he preached to eager converts.

Smiling stone goddesses hint knowledge
  of timeless secrets.
Aegean Sea's sun crystals
  hypnotically beckon travelers,

imploring them to speak of their wonder.
Siren's haunting melody mingles
  with pounding salt spray
    on rocks below.

DISTANT BELLS RING

Feet shuffle through this splendid
chambered room viewing ceiling's
glory. Sounds of awe   air sucked
into lungs while mouth is opened
in silent admiration.

People walk in reverent demeanor
through the chamber with heads directed
upwards. God's Creation of Earth unfolds
upon the Sistine Chapel's painted ceiling.
Michaelangelo skillfully displays his genius

in the tale. Anguished hours spent painting
his brow and neck bent heavenward.
Distant bells ring in praise for the
master in tune with God.

TRAIN RATTLES MY BED

Hourly an old train charged past
  our hotel, whose green shutters hung
    loose against the cracked cement walls.

It loomed high along the edge
  of the foreign sea near railroad crossing.
Balconies sat precariously outside its windows

of this faded gold stucco structure.
  Rhythmic pounding of waves
endlessly wailed with the wind.

Inside my multi-chambered room
  gray barren walls overshadow
the storm raging.

A lone wooden chair rests
  beside the narrow doorway. A ghostly image
of dear friend dressed in white shroud

sits upon this aged throne.
  I wake to the banging of the shutters
as the train rattles my bed. The haunting dream

continues upon each awakening throughout the night.
  Great dread and foreboding shake me
into wakefulness. Great sadness

overtakes my day.
  Upon returning to my home land,
news is received of her death.

PATIO DOOR

We settled into our room
husband, daughter and I. Stepped out onto
eighth floor balcony gazing
at sizzling Mediterranean glare from the

outstretched sea below us. Its brilliance bounced off
glass of patio door. Ships anchored in
bay dotted the horizon. Laughter
danced in the room as we planned our exciting day

while enjoying cappuccino and biscuits. On the balcony
below us, fear and sadness entered riding on
the back of shattering glass and screams.
A young child exuberantly ran

towards the allure of the harbor. Not aware of the glass,
he ran through the patio door.
Terrified sounds startled
our moment of joy.

The sun's rays skipping across the sea
onto our patio   calmed me   as I held
my daughter. Deadly silence seeped upwards
from balcony below.   I reflect on my gratitude.

GONDOLA RIDE

Oh sol la mio the gondolier
sang out across the canal.
Steering us through water ways filled with
floating garbage, we gazed up at walls
of history slowly crumbling.
Cathedrals, Don Juan's palace,
St. Mark's square where violins
serenade patrons enjoying outdoor cafes.
Blessed vino lulled my senses.

Oh sol la mio still rings in my
ears. Feeding infant daughter as we
wound through the ancient
floating city. Passing by a marbled Virgin Mary
holding her infant son, no longer small.
Her eyes searching to heaven.
Nurturing soothes ageless longing.
Rhythmic motion of our gondola lulls
my child and my child within.

FLORIDA

Cypress trees dance to their knees
while white egrets salute the sky.

DRIVE TO SARASOTA BEACH

Relentless flatness fills my vision
  Giant oak trees wave hanging moss
        in the wind.
Cypress trees dance to their knees
  while white egrets salute the sky.

Lost water holes dot ground
  in the haze.
        Long horned Brahmas
stare blankly while
  waiting for the rain.

Alligators lumber inland.
  Cottonmouth stretch in the sun.
        Scattered wild fires send
roaring flames to swallow fir trees.
  I choke on thick smoke in the air.

Relentless flatness leads to soft white sand.
  Aquamarine waves sidle towards sandpipers.
        Rosy blue sky peeks
at water's edge. My delight soars
  while joining pelicans diving into the sea.

ON THE BOARDWALK

On the boardwalk brings
  different images.
Most recently, I have wandered
  the labyrinth of boardwalks
    through swamp and cypress.

Each turn made on the
  worn and splintered wood
    presented a new surprise
      from mother earth's bounty.
Can you hear the ancient cry of wonder?

Geckos scurried pass my feet
  hopping from board to board.
They stood as a statue
  watching me pass, sometimes
    a red blade of skin pulsated from their neck.

Long black snakes slowly flowed
  over knurled cypress knees.
    Large alligator eyes silently watched
      from river below.
Can you hear the ancient cry of wonder?

Turtle backs rose up through green scum-covered
  waterways, stately moss covered
branches leaned over wooden path
  trailing into a timeless wonder.
    Blue Herons loom tall along the way.

White Egrets fish for their dinner,
  snakes hang coiled
    from curved beaks
      glistening in the sun's reflection.
Can you hear the ancient cry of wonder?

I WAS DELIGHTED

I saw a turtle on the road today,
  Mom said, "That's a gopher."
Well, this gopher was digging
  his nails into the pavement
    as he hurried past a mail box.

I'm told those same nails
  dig a hole and call it home.
He stopped to slip into his shell
  when he saw me. I froze in my spot
    watching him slowly gather
      courage to begin again.

A rhythmic beat could be heard
  on hot tar as his feet moved.
He carried his house on his back
  while forging ahead with determination.
    Suddenly, he stopped.

He pooped and then continued
  rhythmic dance on tar.
Surely his load felt lighter now,
  as did my mood.
    I saw a turtle poop on the road today
      and I was delighted.

POLITICAL QUESTIONS

Ruby-stained tears
flow freely
in the rubble
where once
humanity cared.
Now innocence weeps.

A THOUGHT

We spend a lifetime searching for
happiness and security.
While, in truth, they are like
butterflies fluttering before our eyes.

We walk through
the matrix of illusion,
skillfully crafted by our Corporate keepers
conditioning us to live in fear.

We weave our own web
of destruction
called freedom.
Butterflies hover within reach.

TELL ME WHY

the most basic needs
 of humanity
are debated and denied
 repeatedly.

The caveman took better care
 of their clan
then we do for our citizens
 over the world.

Health care isn't an option
 on a form to fill out,
it is a basic need along
 with food and shelter.

Tell me why some people
 are still homeless or
Veterans are forgotten along the way
 with the elderly and the poor.

Citizens still live in trailers years
 after devastating hurricanes.
These concerns are not up for debate or
 politically correct.

They are rights we deserve
 upon birth, yet
we heap people into piles
 of forgotten memories.

Tell me why Power
 is so important
while children huddle eyes huge
 with wonder bellies huge with hunger.

Does it really matter what color
                your skin when President?
What color is your heart
                your soul?

FACES OF TERROR

People fled clouds of smoke
chasing them as they ran
while the towers crumbled.

Flashes of memory from history
brings to mind people fleeing, as Mt. Vesuvius
sent lava flowing through streets of Pompeii.

One disaster created by human hands
flying a vessel into the Trade Center.
Its mission became a human bomb.

Natural disaster became the burial
for thousands in the midst of their life.
Others are put in their grave by hatred.

Faces of terror etched in time.
Fossil remnants are all that remain.
Paying tribute, candle light spreads around
the world.

TODAY

I retreat into
rows of herbs
offered by this garden's maze
stunned

The nation is in mourning
twin towers crumbled
cotton ball clouds float over my sadness
in a massive sea of blueness

Lavender, Oregano,
Rose petals, all send
their fragrance
honoring the missing

in this time of terror
Church bells sound
from many directions
humbly I take in the pain

Your cornucopia of color
cries out for peace
Thank you sweet blossoms
for easing disbelief

CRUISE MISSILES

glide effortlessly
as if they were pelicans
diving for dinner
into the heart of
innocent bystanders.

Ruby-stained tears
flow freely
in the rubble
where once
humanity cared.
Now innocence weeps.

HEALTH CARE

choices for whom? Do politicians
leave their brain
at the door
when they enter the office?

A mother on nightly news
declares her son
should have six grade lessons
not politics.

A wealthy nation
in the 21st Century
has archaic options
for basic care

of its citizens.
Elderly line up
at death's door
and await execution.

Ailing people die
as red tape and loop holes
remain constant
with insurance companies.

Children fall victim
to adult madness.
Maybe it is sanity that was
checked at the door upon entrance.

HOW MANY MORE?

Gunfire echoed off walls
        through windows
                off heads
of children running in terror

How many more will die?

Terrorist explosions echoed through
        crumbling walls of buildings
                of hearts
never to be repaired

How many more will die?

News report tragedies of hate
        refugees of war
                of disaster
bringing unwanted famine into our home

How many more will die?

MASKS

Highway miles burn under truck's weight
it carries life's possessions and,
towed vehicle behind

Pulled into truck stop adding another notch
in the trail of semi's stopped for life support
life's weighted baggage follows my every step

Inside everyone in costume and animated movement
it was a day allowed for masks
different from the others

How many masks do we wear
facing the real reason
we drag our carcass across the country

Along the way, cat dies in my child's arms
I watched the mask of death cloud her eyes
while her body shuttered its last breath

In the sheltered cab we mourn her death
sobbing away masks held tightly
rushing winds from cars passing, echo our sadness

Returning home to original place of pain
slowly the masks are laid to rest
what follows is extreme loneliness

It becomes a window allowing me to see
masks tossed along the way give freedom
to feel with my heart

FACTIONS

Several factions equal the whole
divided by those
preaching absolute Truth.

Can they hear children's footsteps
crunching across hills of garbage
as they search for food?

Each leader assures their people
through scandal and corruption
united we stand, divided we fall.

Tell that to the refugees huddled in camps
around the world as they watch
for a food drop from the sky. Hopelessly

Waiting to quiet their hunger. See the pain
emanating from eyes longing
for freedom and peace sharing a common

Prayer with all nations. The whole world is
watching. Deliberation on policy runs
endlessly on into the night. Morning asks us to

Listen for solutions. Can so many truths
coupled with greed and ruthless killing
ever bring answers to benefit the whole?

Mother Earth nurtures her wounds.
Time demands that we
set aside differences once and for all.

INSANITY RULES

If man is a rational being,
why are there so many
terrorists
criminals
wars

All are watching as the world crumbles
choking, while breathing polluted air
drinking polluted water
eating poisoned food

Is this a result of a rational mind
thinking of its children's future
while committing genocide
of mind and country

Does a rational mind consider
the effects of torture done to someone's
mother
sister
brother

FOLLOW THE RAINBOW

Follow the rainbow to the center
 Where a glorious garden is in bloom
The blue glow of agape power
 Surrounds the Natural child dancing.

The child sings, I want to live
 I want to grow, I want to be
Then stops to look at its reflection
 mirrored from rainbow faces.

I love you, I accept you
 even though I don't understand you.
I love myself, I accept myself
 even though I don't understand myself.

These are words that echo throughout the garden
 A safe place where we met, led by angels
Our tears covered that heavy sack we carry
 Its content are years of self-doubt and fear.

Illumination made way for celebration
 Light held high from under that bushel
I am responsible to myself
 I no longer wear the mask of responsibility for others.

I am grateful for these rainbow faces
 who have the courage to be
We join hands in the guided journey, while singing
 It's about time we realize we're all in this together.

EPILOGUE

"Jesus replied: "Fear not Albion: unless I died thou canst
not live;
But if I die I shall rise again & thou with me.
This is Friendship & Brotherhood: without it Man
Is Not."....

Albion reply'd: "Cannot Man exist without Mysterious
Offering of Self for Another: is this Friendship &
Brotherhood?
I see thee in the likeness and similitude of Los (God) my
Friend."

Jesus said: "Wouldest thou love one who never died
For thee, or ever died for one who had not died for
thee?

And if God dieth not for Man & giveth not himself
Eternally for Man, Man could not exist; for Man is
Love
As God is Love; every kindness to another is a little
Death
In the Divine Image, nor can Man exist but by
Brotherhood."

William Blake, "Jerusalem"

ABOUT THE AUTHOR

Elaine Webster is from the Rochester, NY area. She graduated from the University of Buffalo, received her AMS Montessori Teaching Certificate from AERCO in Philadelphia, PA and attended classes at Writers & Books. Elaine has worked at a variety of different places throughout her life including Planned Parenthood, a Drug and Alcohol Clinic and for the Head Start Program in the inner city. She also worked with the elderly for six years, which compelled her to write her second book entitled, "Grandma's in the Basement." Her many travels throughout the US, Canada, Italy and Greece helped inspire her work. Elaine enjoys being a mother, teacher, artist and is presently working on her next book.

www.ingramcontent.com/pod-product-compliance
Lightning Source LLC
LaVergne TN
LVHW091010080826
845145LV00003B/1204
* 9 7 8 1 9 3 3 5 6 7 2 8 0 *